Gallery Books
Editor: Peter Fallon

MARCONI'S COTTAGE

Medbh McGuckian

MARCONI'S COTTAGE

Gallery Books

Marconi's Cottage
is first published
simultaneously in paperback
and in a clothbound edition
on 28 November 1991.

The Gallery Press
Loughcrew
Oldcastle
County Meath
Ireland

ISBN 1 85235 081 4 (*paperback*)
     1 85235 082 2 (*clothbound*)

The Gallery Press receives financial assistance from An Chomhairle
Ealaíon / The Arts Council, Ireland, and acknowledges also the assistance of the Arts Council of Northern Ireland in the publication of this
book.

Contents

View without a Room *page* 9
Visiting Rainer Maria 10
The Invalid's Echo 12
The Man with Two Women 14
To Call Paula Paul 16
Springwater 20
Dear Rain 22
The Liontamer 24
Journal Intime 26
Brothers and Uncles 27
Shaferi 29
A Small Piece of Wood 31
The Cutting-Out Room 33
Gigot Sleeves 35
The Sun-Moon Child 37
The Most Emily of All 38
No Streets, No Numbers 39
Road 32, Roof 13-23, Grass 23 42
The Cloth Mother 44
The Keeper Ring 45
The Book Room 46
A Test Winter 48
A Different Same 49
Clotho 50
Dormer Window 52
The Watch Fire 53
The Rosary Dress 55
Amsterdam Avenue 57
The Unplayed Rosalind 59
Lac de Galance 62
East of Mozart 64
Echo-Poem 67
The Partner's Desk 70
Swallows' Wood, Glenshesk 72
Storm-Flap 74

Turning the Moon into a Verb 76
Earth Weather 77
Branches 78
Sky-Writing 79
Open Rose 80
Venus and the Sea 81
The War Ending 82
Charlotte's Delivery 83
Breaking the Blue 84
Oval of a Girl 85
From the First Underworld 86
The Carrying Ring 88
The After-Thinker 90
Almond 91
She Which Is Not, He Which Is 93
Vibratory Description 95
In the Rainshadow 96
Flowered Sitting-room 98
The Snow Speaker 99
Sky in Narrow Streets 100
Red Armchair 102
Marconi's Cottage 103
Teraphim 104
Time-Words 106
On Her Second Birthday 107

Acknowledgements and Notes 110

*for Barbara Jahrling
and Anne Ulry Colman*

View without a Room

My bones are painted two shades of red
Like the bones of a salmon. If you belong
To the second of these you will always
Be in love with the first. I threw sand
As far inland in you as I could get, my eyes
Like dried flowers splitting into finer
And finer hairs, where it was the essence
Of the earth to light the moon: are
You like a dream in fact, able to take
The next step, and shape yourself like
A fold-out bed of bones, like an actual
House I know, where everything was under a spell
And sure to form itself into a circle?

Your first name is a woman's, your last name
Is a boy's, and when I asked you how you would
Choose to kill yourself, winter or drowning,
You said you were a citizen that knows
The sea only from the beach. There is
No single reason for most of your sleep
Being dream, or for the blood-long race
Of your talk, when thunder passes into you
His voice, data, image and text.
I am a brush strapped to your hand,
A sunset beard on your skin, and it is
Not downwards, from the light, but
Slowly upwards, from the dark, before
My five-minute dream can begin.

Visiting Rainer Maria

He said he was just leaving
As I was just arriving, in my blue
Smock, yesterday, without meaning to.
Though this first sentence would
Have been equally suitable
For the last, for a poem made
From a kitchen conversation.

The air was the way it always
Is in a room; books lay in ruins
On the snow-cold bed. He must have been
Scrubbing the floor with his toothbrush,
Using his shoulder as an ashtray,
From the kind of insanity running
Through the American shadow furnishings.

So was my shape dictated by
The curved outer wall, the eccentricities
Of the corridor, all sorts of untils.
And I thought to myself, if he touches
My sleeve even softly, whole streets
Of shops near the sea will be extinguished
In the most intentional darkness:

If he mentions a river it will be one
Renouncing the moon, that lends itself
To a foreglimpse of the day's
Callisthenics, stirring into animal storm,
Adding a feminine ending to
Whatever parts are dream. Of the place,
It was godforsaken; of the season, dead;

But whether it was sea or flesh,
Short capsules of conscripted
Cooling wax were laid like expiry

Dates over partings of quite a different
Cast. I said, I must find it,
Using the feminine form of must,
What *you* want, what *I* want, what can be done.

For four more virgin months I have been
Not his, *not* his, *not* his, *his*,
A sea-kitten rolling up in his
English shirt like a tray of Persian
Tea, neutral as a cloud. Because
The *it* of his translation may mean silence,
But the *she* of mine means Aphrodite.

The Invalid's Echo

It was as if he put a thermometer
Back in its holder without shaking it,
Or snatched a cigarette out of my mouth
Like a secret breath, the way he put
His finger on the rest, and we were disconnected.

The thinnest paper was an unbidden blue,
That had summoned him (it took five calls),
Sitting behind a desk, waking him
Prematurely, as a parent-poem,
Out of an unfrightened, ten-year stretch
Of love, for twenty minutes by an open window.

His foliage was unlike that of any other,
His sound was like nothing else, my ears
Were never rested; I would have spent
The rest of my life felling his timber,
Never taking my eyes off him,
Always looking straight at his mouth,
If that was how he liked it.

He practises at death with each embrace;
In the language of our grandmothers,
Who spoke God's name continually,
Forgotten by our own free will,
He says a prayer for the dying over
Himself and me; his endearments
Execute the house's deepest reds.

A house heals easily, blood shed
In the past loses its hue; if I could die
The same death in the same air
As him, I would wish my grave
Untended too, like everybody else's;

Like the bulb that has not been washed
Since the revolution, the hole
In the ceiling that has left
A little pile of plaster on the floor.

I think his family is so ancient,
His heart must still be over on the right,
Though I have searched for it before
In full swing until it shrank to nothing,
Merging with my name, that comes
From nowhere, and is ownerless,
Like all we can see of the stars.

Now, like them, I lie with my back
To him, his chance neighbour,
Watching the entrance to the house,
But not the house. The long autumn
Has scattered its poisonous seeds,
So I will have no October child.

By the time I have the dream
That he will seek the word
With his fingers — the word that can
Scarcely be used — that having forgotten
Everything he will imagine the sky
In its second appearance as
The quintessence of blue,

I will be freezing in my short jacket.
In my last dream it was after January;
I was buying food for him when
A truck I have lost track of
Came rattling into the overfulfilled courtyard.

The Man with Two Women

I'd been walking
                on a very old street
Leading to the sea,
                    to a gritty beach
With huge stones,
                where I would sit
In a stylish sundress,
                    laced boots and pearls,
Re-reading five, ten times,
                        the simplest letters
From people who lived there
                        and emigrated.

It was a hopelessly
                ill-advised summer,
One of a hundred
                bizarre days,
Of lip-cutting wind
                and gold-enclosed
Irish clouds,
                rocking their past
In their arms as if
                they were still in their
Army uniforms with
                the shoulder-tabs removed.

My tired skin
                was letting the rain
Get inside the halves
                of my collar when
He entered as he
                would his own home,
Placing himself
                there in the square

Like a monument
                    and suddenly,
In the doorway,
                    pulling off his shirt.

Though I never promised
                            my long kiss
To anyone,
                    he turned his yard-wide
Shoulders as if
                    harnessed, like a
Grand piano,
                    suspended upside-
Down, over
                    my head.

I could have
                    edged the breeze,
Never within a house,
                                to pour sand
Into his mouth,
                        but getting dark
Is the world's fault:
                            Send me
My winter.

To Call Paula Paul

for Brenda McKeown

Winter begins the way no one ever
Moves. I have postponed her now
To Friday, till I have thrown
Autumn's image on a
Heap of smouldering leaves.

She did not arrive uninvited,
More than invited; her narrow
Mouth pleased me, the ideas
Inside it. I received her
In a sleeveless frock,
A significance above daylight,
A twin of April who might bring
A softer light to bear
On what the wind didn't dry.

Since she was water-shy, we
Embraced only in doorways and on the sea-
Wall, the safe balcony
With its frayed chairs, while
The heavy light lay solid,
Golden, on the heavy, white sand.
At night she fell diagonally
Into my bed like ripe
Fruit, or a waterless river.

If you want to picture me,
I am lying full length, on my back,
As though a woman were carrying
Me (this is my way of sleeping
Off bad news), as though my soft,
Pink, rented carpet were following
The music of my mother-to-be dreams,

Keeping close to the walls, listening
With outstretched fingers as a bed never will.

In these discreeter lights, well satisfied
With rain and uncertainty, I dissect again
My Christmas cards for 1934, side by side
At their workless desks, a windowful of faces
Slides away, and smells of emptiness,
Like the breeze that forced itself
Through a conspicuous eyelet in her dress.

I did nothing, I didn't cry;
I held the permanent bangle on her wrist
For a long time. In the bright July
My window seemed too big, all day
Long to insult me, with its pale heaven,
Putting supple hands around my throat.

Our hearts were all beating on
The far left, something was starting
At the top of her left breast,
To furnish it ironically. I touched
Her foot with mine; also I shook
My head at the mirror, all
Blotches and ripples, the dark
Marks symmetrically dividing
Up her face, as if from deep snow,
Suddenly a sordid light
Was sent up into a warm room.

The wind is at its cruellest at breakfast;
It has mouths, it outshouts me,
It knocks cameras out of newspapermen's
Haphazard hands, it makes sure
Books get torn during arguments.

In the film-like freedom
Of its movement, it blows
The puppet clouds through a key.

Most children have theatre in them,
My one-child audience smiles
Like a deck-chair unrelaxed, some
Hoped-for person with too-white a face,
The blue-black hedge of her shadowless
Eyes absorbing nothing of this different
Light of seven o'clock in the morning,
The half-height curtains,
The house-lights left on.

I hear her voice like a telephone
Torn from the wall by lightning
Where she is telephoning endlessly.
The house is too pretty, the air
Is tasteless, there are no seasons yet.

In the typewriter, very thin paper
Is folded double — it has been
Lifted out of the century.
The bloodless flowers draw
Attention to her breast, where
I look for a little price tag
On that curious rustling 'R'
In my mornings.

So many orange skies have smashed
The light bulbs of the weather,
I look critically at the completely
Missing week. If you are changing
Trains by starlight, darling,
Wear a white tie deluded by

A white shirt, for when I called
Him 'bought', I only wounded him;
They're *his* soldiers, *his* lorries,
Recruiting ghosts in your street tonight.

Springwater

for Nuala Ní Dhomhnaill

Her kisses are so light,
You have to kiss her, and kiss her,
The last one is the one
To be pitied.

The dew, to which you may
Be a stranger, is the stain
Which has seeped from the middle
To the very edge of the cloth.

Which is the natural place
To begin, with dawn
At your disposal, cut in half
Lengthwise, and through it

A grey ribbon slightly
Off-centre, running towards
The sound of firing.
I would part with a girl

Before a rifle, but I forbid
Her slow mouth to everyone,
Her fingers so curiously
Under your breath.

I press the italics of her soul
Between yours and mine,
Till her throat whitens
And ovarian fountains

Gush out of openings
They have made for themselves.
My desecrated hearth
Is of the brown shade

Which rather suits
The spice of that feeling:
How parasol intertwines
With complexion, rosewater, far.

Dear Rain

I have seen men with the colouring
Of the torso of this heavy day (of time
Stolen from sleep) and felt the Irishness
Of my face (less than ever mine)
Settle into a cloud of bitter bone.

But one journey — one man — washes out
Another; and a clear evening turns
Its cadaverous cocoon in front of me
Like a book-lined room or a child
Simply forgetting to hate.

I left the winter for a man who liked
Light, who bent towards the murdered
Past as a sunflower and did not talk
Of victory. I knew he was there
At the very moment I knew he was not.

I thought, so natural a voice should not
Be allowed lightly to dissolve. He seemed
To be a skein of dreams walking;
He did not like talk
To have its North and South.

The background in which
His language made sense made
His light voice lighter and himself
An outward light, a night-long
Splendid summer.

Though he was dead, in the room
There were always flowers,
And the stair still turned
In the house as sleeplessly
As time.

Once it is long enough over
It is only his language they understand,
Not what he was trying to say:
But I
Had cried out my promise in his unconscious

Ear, fatal as the first run, safe against
The worst guilt, a jealous husband,
I would be his second spring, his any hope
Of another, no less innocent, surrender
To midnight, to winter, or to wine.

The Liontamer

Two mirrors in one room are like a double
Kiss, more-than-daily letters sent
In a double envelope. At a given hour
She pours out a view of trees and sky,
Her eyes intent upon forty thousand houses.
Between five and six her head will do
Whatever you wish. She will serve you
The new fruit glistening with rain,
And coffee crushed to a mocha flood,
So sleep will be a tongue to keep
Your cheated flesh going — so sleep
Will never talk to you as an owner.

Over the thirty nights of this month,
A thin rain borrowed my silver, took
Something of me with him, now
An enormous river draining near the sea.
I kept my watch in my hand, as if
I had only twenty minutes, on a blue
Ribbon, a strip torn from a gown of blue
And white she had worn on the first day;
Moulded to her, as she moulded perfectly
To you, pitch-dark and flexible as silk.

Why should you worry in that bright setting
If the price of her favours was the expulsion
Of the English, or she aged twenty years
In the month, steep and ungrateful as the soil
You drain around you like a tree? You wipe
A cup and then kiss where her signature
Disappears from the paper. You rejoice
That twenty years should occupy
So little space, within a yard of you,
And not exactly fit the mould, the
Rich curves of a twenty-seven year old heart.

A pallor has overtaken the brown marble
Tiles, overmoist, half-covered with full-
Lipped flowers, that begin again in the tapestry

Frame and the foot of the rug, only there
They are meagre clumps of lilac — in the
Pansy-coloured curtained bassinet.
Love me for a year, and you will see
My denial of flowers is an attachment for
White; that in doing none of the things
Done by other women, the blue of my
Weather fights the cloud of your voice.
And you know how real a cloud is, you
With your liontamer's eyes, their gold flecks
A thousand infatuations and repentances,
Their panes like a flight of clouds

In a windowed passageway. I have thought
Of their small contractions when I was crying,
Or quiet, at one- or two-monthly intervals,
When the glass-paned door lighted the room
Into a picture without a frame, a frame
Without a picture. I saw you as a lake,
I dined on your sap as on a sound fruit.
Just now, I found myself making that
Smothered movement with my arms *she* made
When she was preoccupied with her skirt,
Or swathing herself in your male cloak,
Closing the last circle of herself.

Journal Intime

In the dreams of men the pattern
Of the wallpaper by moonlight
Is the death-devoted colour of masculinity.
And in artfully-placed mirrors,
A single, grieving shape, to the
Weak-eyed, echoes and re-echoes,
More than sister, more than wife.

Red is the colour of art and of the
True centre of the summer
Whose gestures endanger the carpet's
New nimbleness and heat, trapping
Shadows, dissipating all the pauses
Of the day and night. It is
A two-faced fruit, a lifelong winter.

I am a Platonic admirer of her
Flowing, Watteau gowns, the volume
Of Petrarch in her lap. It is so
Unthinkable she should look outward
From the depressed, pink light of her
One-time nursery, if only to dilate
Upon the same two faces, if only, upon the snow.

In a child's first (and most satisfying)
House, where everyone is repeated
In everyone else, the door that is so light
To her, so dark to us, is wise enough
To dream through. Her voice fills the mouth
Of her own mirror, as if she were a failure:
As if, what is lifelike, could be true.

Brothers and Uncles

These days called 'nature', I write with my eyes
Shut to the male sky and its most common clouds.
Their whiteness is not an invitation, their whiteness
Has not chosen me, the egg of the weather is down,
Like the neck of an old bottle, or a sometime mistress.

Winter was a page that asked to be written on:
I asked for her fatigue to be removed, her broad foot,
Her falling lip, her broad thumb, that heavy weight
Laid across me, my truest and darkest double,
Her large-limbed books, her soundless slippers, her dryness.

The stone of a room will digest the half-bared
Moonlight, half-a-house the cold of some stars;
But I saw my wish outside me like a shawl,
Like a wall, tinged like a blush, light as a child,
That is calmed by plaiting her waist-length hair.

A scarlet-draped window-seat, shaped to echo
The circular mirror, itself a sort of chamber, adorned
The parlour, like a moon where we spilt the needles'
Fertile grey powder, like a sleep or a pregnancy,
Over the wooden-backed sofa which doubled as a bed.

As she herself might have wished to be overheard,
Her unseduceable, two rows of small, black doors,
Her shimmering abstention from summers as a shirt
That might weaken its wearer: a plain woman,
Not a secret knife that cannot be housed.

Or a black and white sky, split into neighbouring
Rooms, their wet weather bringing strong dreams,
That never join or touch, like a wedding on board
A ship, spoken without a book. Easter is
Her home, all colour is the air of her country.

And what uncolours it, what shrinks the mended
Width of her dawn-fires, is those muselike bundles,
The snowstorm I described to you six men ago,
When I fastened myself open like a grave
Or even more like a house, for the wrong man.

Shaferi

Ten simple mistakes: a song thrush?
A mistle thrush? Perhaps it was late
Summer and I remembered the burning
Brown of its polished trees as autumn,
Or there was half-an-hour less bird-watching
Sun slipping into my skin. All those letters
About handkerchiefs (meaning passports);
All those code-names for towns beginning
With cooler initials; all the substituting
Of women's lives for men's; I plucked them
Out of the network of the war-time mail
To the most closely-watched place
In the Empire, and turned them
As he turned the plates so the double-headed
Eagle faced the diner. Like the nerves
Of my favourite sea that lets the beauty
Of its scented, dark eyes soak into me,
Or the newlywed, champagne tiles
He reverently painted with starfish,
Shells and beech-leaf red anemones:
It wasn't true when he said it,
'Love is of the body'; it *became* true
Later on, one winding and the other
Unwinding, when it became unspoken,
As my copper ring, fatigued, tightened
In my baggy pocket into a book-shaped
Brooch. Which was an ominous
Address for it: two rooms at the corner
Of Gendarme and Prison Street, where
Even the smallest stone like an overfull
Heart can refuse to do its job. A stone
From my soul marks the first day
Of change: the desk, that is a table,

At which I am sewing gold stars
Into a skirt, forms a not-quite
Semi-circle of pine.

A Small Piece of Wood

On the secret shelves of weather,
With its few rhymes, in a pause
Of blood, I closed the top
Of my lesson-filled inkwell,
A she-thing called a poetess,
Yeoman of the Month.

In pale frock and raspberry
Boots, my waist the circumference
Of no more than two oranges,
I rode out to hunt, with my
White linen eyes and my lips
Cut out of a piece of red material.

On my left two rivers flowed
Together without mingling,
As though someone had unrolled
Two different ribbons side by side,
Or three-quarters of the sky, allowed
To touch, but not to mix, with winter.

The sweepings of my study
Seemed all spoiled remnants
In which the colour had run,
As if the hook of a clasp
Had got from eyelet to eyelet
Till it could unbuckle no further.

Pictures in children's books used
To be painted in by children,
Each with a silent pen, a guide,
Seated round a table, each a colour
To himself, wherever it appeared,
No one child a whole picture.

While my numberless blues
Have neither end nor beginning,
Arranged like a tribe of lovers
In a circle — my headdress
A flaxen wig, a velvet bandeau,
A beaver hat, with a plume of feathers

Dropped from the neck and breast
Of a black-winged stilt:
Every apple is a feather-room
For seed's infectious star, and every man
Who calls a woman 'Choorka',
For a hundred and eight ruled pages.

The Cutting-Out Room

Light, like a defect, cut the rain.
The legal daylight held
Its starshaped umbrella over me.
And people said, the weather *will* hold,
As if they tied it up in a bag for me.

I had on my youngest, speedwell blouse —
The sleeves are full at the top,
Caught in at the elbow, then
Full again — like a belt slackened
Around your head, or being emptied

From bottle to bottle. I had
Smoothed the cream of youth, or manhood,
Into my arms, my body, the kiss
Of a spent-salmon where
The earth is never wet.

Your eyes were like thatch
When moss grows over it; your
Woman-thirst like a stripe of sun
On the second blue plate; your voice,
A strange swoop of sound, as from

A room above a shop, your hands
As if I glimpsed them in shallow,
Running water, though you would call it
Swimming in as heavy
A sea as you could find.

One month in the best year,
The sun comes through that window,
A year's rain is a phial
Of white blood drying inwardly
In the moon-shaped air:

My neck against the pillow
Of the claret carpet would have been
A field trained to draw — if
I had not said 'if' before,
I would have said it after that;

I am saying it now.

Gigot Sleeves

There are bibles left about the house:
Here is the bible open, here is the bible shut,
A spreading here, a condensation there.

The double-cherry performs a dance behind
Triple gauze, she takes out the bulldogs,
Masters a pistol, sleeps on a camp bed

Without a fireplace or curtain, in the
Narrow sliproom over the front hall —
A woman-sized, un-beringed, inexact fit.

When she hears the wheels of his carriage,
She blows out the candle, she does not yearn
For the company of even a lamp.

For a gown-length, she chooses
A book-muslin patterned with lilac
Thunder and lightning. Her skirts

Are splashed with purple suns, the sleeves
Set in as they used to be fifteen years
Ago. If she takes up a piece of sewing,

She will be shirt-making; in a laundry-book
She writes as though fifteen hundred Englishmen
Had been slaughtered just beyond the garden,

Or it was there Trelawney threw the frankincense
And salt into the fire, poured the wine
And oil over the wave-worn depths of Shelley.

Her petticoats have neither curve nor wave
In them, the whole depth of the house,
Like a secret tie between a wound and its weapon.

And everything is emaciated — the desk
On her knees, the square of carpet, the black
Horsehair sofa, and the five-foot-seven by sixteen

Inches, of a pair of months, stopped.

The Sun-Moon Child

I dreamt I could make from the summer
A winter childbirth, by turning the slats
Of a window to darken a room in Italy.
The house was impossibly fragile, made
Of cloth and glass, the room floated freely
Within itself, and the bed was let into
A recess, like a stitch that is slack and loose.

My dress was gun-metal grey, with a blow-away
Hem: I had saved up my money in an old,
Shoulder-length evening glove, and the third
And fifteenth of every month were our first meeting,
Our first night. Sleep hammered out the days
Within the bounds of an hour; I accepted the dream's
Standpoint and decision, like a false season.

His skin and hair and eyes were cloaked
In the warm tones of the day, so he was an Adam
Of the young dead of World War One,
Or Satan, in the shape of a star-jessamine,
Who cursed by name the moon and its perfume.
The clouds had space to travel the grey
Background of his seven-minute flame,

Until the cherry-spotted bed to the right
Of the Spanish Steps became
A blanket of chance-gathered roses
For Keats's first night in the grave.
When I thought out my dream, it was some days
Old, a cluster of half-rooms with Austrian blinds,
And no France; it was the hundredth birthday
Of my name grandmother.

The Most Emily of All

When you dream wood I dream water.
When you dream boards, or cupboard,
I dream a lake of rain, a race sprung
From the sea. If you call out 'house' to me
And I answer 'library', you answer me
By the very terms of your asking,
As a sentence clings tighter
Because it makes no sense.

Your light hat with the dark band
Keeps turning up; you pull it right
Down over your head and run the fingers
Of your right hand up and down
In a groove on the door panel. A finger
Going like this into my closed hand
Feels how my line of life turns back
Upon itself, in the kind of twilight
Before the moon is seen.

A verse from a poem by Lermentov
Continually goes round
In my head. A full ten days
Has elapsed since I started my
'You can go or stay' letter, increasingly
Without lips like the moon that night,
A repercussive mouth made for nothing,
And used for nothing.
Just let me moisten your dreamwork
With the lower half of the letter,
Till my clove-brown eyes beget a taller blue.

No Streets, No Numbers

for Janice Fitzpatrick

The wind bruises the curtains' jay-blue stripes
Like an unsold fruit or a child who writes
Its first word. The rain tonight in my hair
Runs a firm, unmuscular hand over something
Sand-ribbed and troubled, a desolation
That could erase all memory of warmth
From the patch of vegetation where torchlight
Has fallen. The thought that I might miss
Even a second of real rain is like the simple
Double knock of the stains of birth and death,
Two men back to back carrying furniture
From a room on one side of the street
To a room on the other. And the weather
Is a girl with woman's eyes like a knife-wound
In her head. Such is a woman's very deep
Violation as a woman; not like talk,
Not like footsteps; already a life crystallises
Round it; and time, that is so often only a word,
'Later, later', spills year into year like three days'
Post, or the drawing-room with the wall
Pulled down.

I look into the endless settees
Of the talk-dried drawing-room where all
The colours are wrong. Is that because
I unshaded all the lamps so their sunny,
Unhurt movements would be the colour
Of emotions which have no adventures?
But I'm afraid of the morning most,
Which stands like a chance of life
On a shelf, or a ruby velvet dress,
Cut to the middle of the back,
That can be held on the shoulder by a diamond lizard.

A stone is nearly a perfect secret, always
By itself, though it touches so much, shielding
Its heart beyond its strong curtain of ribs
With its arm. Not that I want you
To tell me what you have not told anyone:
How your narrow house propped up window
After window, while the light sank and sank.
Why your edges, though they shine,
No longer grip precisely like other people.
How sometimes the house won, and sometimes
The sea-coloured, sea-clear dress,
Made new from one over a hundred years old,
That foamed away the true break
In the year, leaving the house
Masterless and flagless. That dream
Of a too early body undamaged
And beautiful, head smashed to pulp,
Still grows in my breakfast cup;
It used up the sore red of the applebox,
It nibbled at the fortnight of our violent
Christmas like a centenarian fir tree.

I talk as if the evenings had been fine,
The roof of my shelves not broken
Like an oath on crossed rods,
Or I had not glimpsed myself
As the Ides of September, white
At the telephone. Two sounds
Spin together and fight for sleep
Between the bed and the floor,
An uneasy clicking-to of unsorted
Dawn-blue plates, the friction
Of a skirt of hands refusing to let go.
And how am I to break into
This other life, this small eyebrow,

Six inches off mine, which has been
Blown from my life like the most aerial
Of birds? If the summer that never burnt,
And began two days ago, is ashes now,
Autumn's backbone will have the pallor
Of the snowdrop, the shape of the stone
Showing in the wall. Our first summer-time
Night, we will sit out drinking
On the pavement of Bird Street,
Where we kissed in the snow, as the day
After a dream in which one really was
In love, teases out the voice reserved for children.

Road 32, Roof 13-23, Grass 23

The dark wound her chestnut hair
Around her neck like the rows of satin trimming
On a skirt with three flounces.
She pressed firmly down the sides of her eyes
The colour of the stem of the wild geranium
And of the little ball holding the snowdrop petals.

In winter she dreamt the back views
Of young men on high ladders, their fingers
Through bookcases like hummingbirds,
Radiating for miles into the forest.
Her water-loving fern liked the rain
Down her back and the sun coming in early

Going round the house slamming doors.
One morning a week she arranged a jug
Of tomato-coloured blooms face to face
In the exact centre of the table.
She did not light the lamp or the fire,
Though he lit a station of candles

In wine bottles for their first kiss;
The candlelight left a film of woodsmoke
Over everything. Her fear of light began
While his coat still hung over a chair,
The window seemed a picture eased out of her,
She had not wanted her own face there.

'Use the other door' — he shut the ever-open
Door behind his doubly-closed face
With the air of a wasted afternoon
Or an occasional gasp that filled
The house, to be scraped off
Afterwards like a point of purple ribbon.

She slept with his letter in her hand,
And the longest letter she wrote
Was on the back of his letter
To a woman who never existed.

But sat on her midsummer doorstep
Dusted with wood ash like a letter,
Or the icy rain, stoked with
Fallen boughs, on her coverlet.

The Cloth Mother

I sat where the women sat, a thrift pink
Farm-wife; the woodland greens of my dress
Suggested a wheatfield crawling with poppies.

The leaves were so stiff they might have been wired.
The rain was the size of almonds; in the lukewarmth,
Richard sang to the small of my back, 'O promise me'.

We looked well interlocked, I tended the eighteen
Lamps when the sky drained too light a turquoise,
The house seemed to rise in the air and curtsey.

Later, I played I was my own daughter for a year;
I designed a many-pocketed beaded dress for her
So she could sense the spark of her skeleton.

I reshelved her books, old and new; I produced more
Dreams for her than if I had lived in sixty houses,
To make her feel as framed and central as a night

Without a dream. I searched for her full breasts,
Circles within the circles of her clothes, and empty-handed
Gave her my idea of the lowest kiss; not a kiss

Like a kiss, but as if you were really looking
In somebody's eyes. I never get halfway to orange
In my doorless, stepless dreams,

So she must have thought what the unconceived
Catch in my voice meant, how weak the edge
Of my rain-softened hair.

In the next time-band, the day
With her palms up wears a white accent
And nothing but *Je Reviens*.

The Keeper Ring

My eyes change in the direction of the gentlest brown.
Yours are all the shapes that the blackbird's egg shows.
The rain is an open display on the emptiness of my lips;
Sweet because odourless, it muzzles into everything.

The roads between us are ill-lit; the traffic islands,
The telephone kiosks, the cruising areas have less reality
Than the equator, like a face suggesting movement
No less than a bird's wings. Yours is a side of life

I've not lain on, though once I leaned out of bed
And stretched my arm to within an inch of the base
Of your sleeping throat, as if willing you to wake.
This dark house we had planned to leave

Carries a single letter on its back, the floor raying
Out in lozenge greens and two pairs of leaves, as though
In its world there were no autumn. The hollyhocks
Decapitated, swim in a basin chased with four birds;

Each tress on the mantelpiece fringe is plaited
Into four strands, at the end of each a little golden
Ball. You fold your napkin into the packed muscles
Of a millefeuilles, I stir my spoon into the French-grey

Lining of my cup, till it is reborn in the blue-
Embroidered saucer of its nest. The house dreams
In the skip of my sentence, flame-coloured now, Italian-
Walled, though the snow-fed light passes one tree only.

The Book Room

I know this room so well
I can't walk through it.

Three deep windows, all south,
Their shapes dark clots on the carpet.

Fruit and daffodil curtains
With a bit cut out and pinned together.

Flame has passed over the warm house-wall,
Leaving a touch of red in the cheek.

A waistless vase on a small white mat,
Her skirt pulled up over her bodice.

The bluebell petals almost touch, almost polish,
The grey that is so kind as you come in,

A boy-like, thin, soprano line of soulless bone
Like a bangle round the hand of the ceiling.

The green sofa shell-shaped, scooped out of stone,
Or a farm set into the earth, a comb

Drawn all the length of the hair.
I know those steps, that folded cloud shade

Is a web of torn sea, a balustrade
Threaded through with sea, like thread-

Gloves or sand shoes. A letter breaking
The bounds of letters. A sea

That sounds like an island sea.
A rain that is not a winter or an August rain.

A sky that is a whole where light flies
Like a bird. I lie on my right side

And put my hand up to my forehead,
While he looks out of his window,

And I look out of mine.

A Test Winter

Spring skims the garden with his wintry eyes,
Their electric-blue centres stained
With a little pale blood
So they look brown in photographs.

I hear the ghost of that harsh voice printed
On the empty spaces of my answering-machine.
I see him put the tips of his fingers together,
In a steeple, two birds, one on each
Of my shoulders.

Now the trees' swaying summits meet,
Now swing aside, and I wish you and I
Had been beautiful, such pine-knots,
Large as a walnut, small as an apple.

A rope of female imagery presses
A below-zero nerve, till her hair springs
In twenty parallel partings,
The buds of black infibulated roses.

Framed in a doorway, she makes herself
A serving-hatch, one hip unswept
And jutted out. Her long stem
Makes this a test winter.

My own first lesson was on the wrist,
The china cupboard of its tendons where
One cup arranged for every woman who ever loved
The stammerer, to stammer in her speech.

A Different Same

Moonlight is the clearest eye:
Moonlight as you know enlarges everything.
It occupies a pool so naturally
It might have grown there.
Its stoniness makes stones look less than us.
Our hands begin to feel like hooves
Deep in this life and not in any other.
It can free the crossed arms from the body
Where time has fitted them without question,
And place them once random in a swimming
Position, so it seems you have opened
Without sound. There are figures standing
On steps, and figures reading. Not one
Walks past without being blurred
Like bronze snapshots. The church bell hangs
In the swirling porthole of the yew tree,
Pierced by a sea as abstract and tough
As the infant around the next corner.
Morning, mid-morning, afternoon and evening,
The rose that is like a pink satin theatre
Programme spreads to three gardens
With her roots in one. Her gaze, from the intersection
Of the terrace, gathers in the horizon,
A ceiling of translucent planes
With paintings of fruit in each. Awake at night
Uprooted me from some last minute shoulder.
I came out of the photograph
With that year underneath this dream;
It met with his mouth.

C

Clotho

Music is my heroine, the synthetic kisses
Of a woman's body. Drop by drop
She distilled them, I watched the non-togetherness
Of her sweetish old-maid lips,
Her trained and pocket-mouthed smile.

Like the shadow of an aeroplane
With but one side of wings,
She moved parallel to me,
Leaving the air unflown.

My arms were stretched as high
And wide as they could go,
A distaff reaching from heaven to earth.
But there was nothing to burn
My tongue on, not even a broken stalk
Of lilac-veined sound behind her broken eyes.

Blue does not describe them, they were
A blue and silver room
That sent me half-filled away.
I dropped three-quarters
Of my words for I did not need them.

They should be another colour,
There should be black swans,
Though a satellite is never
Anything but feminine, and crawls
Under your pillow
Because of the horror of touch.

There should be a darkness
Which is anything but death,
Not the false daylight of the stage,

The most expensive white
Of all those pairs of hands
Born for a few sealed railway trains,
All of which were dead by morning.

In just these moments it has grown dark,
And the moon, the semi-human,
Radioactive moon, is at a diagonal
Past childbearing, neither lying down
Nor sitting, since this
Is a flowerless month.

I am possessed of such strength
That I knock down my servant,
My house god, my all-powerful
Mistress of tone, and her moan
Comes clear-cut from another world,
As if translating.

Dormer Window

for Bernadette Ross

The kisses that we kiss are a new
Part of me, their smaller life like
Eight bridesmaids, four in blue,
Four in red. I uttered the word
Beautiful, I spoke of atmosphere,
'So original, so like a seashell'.

He said the bookstrewn light was real light,
He broke off a spray of beech
To exploit every leaf of the future
Autumn, when the sky would be unseen.
I had the primrose-coloured desire
To draw an ideal corner of his head,

Or drop my head into the invisible
Bronze of his throat. If I saw him
Every day most of the day and
Got used to those eyes, I would
Not be sorry enough. The only kind
Of love I'm capable of

Is the strictly human yesterday
Of a right hand tied up and
Covered. A rose-laden dinner party
Swells up and stands like a wave
Of B-flat minor; in all the doyleys
With red borders I undo the knot.

The Watch Fire

i.m. Brian Rothwell

Perhaps no one ever needed this
More than I,
I had stretched out my hand for it
So often.

When spring hesitates
We must wait for it,
Orion's chair is vacant at the table,
Though I had already loosened it.

On the tile oven
In the chimney room,
I brew warm milk with herbs
For my knowledge of the sky,
I am so frightened
When it begins to throb again.

A strange ring
Gives out heat like a lit window:
Now it seems too large
For my finger, now it fits perfectly,
Its stone fizzes up in joy
And seems to give me
Some kind of answer.

Suddenly man is nothing
And the stone everything,
I contract
And rinse you off my heart,
And consecrate my sleep to the rain
And all that goes with it.

Then I offer you my lips
Like an ointment, a calendar
Between now and a year from now,
When the identical
Childbed hangings will be dotted
With intentional, identical
Blue cubes.

The Rosary Dress

A white armless dress, a cloak of roses,
A coat of morning as August grows.
I must install myself inside that seed,
I, and my weight of stars.

When the vine dies, the colour imprisoned
Inside the olive tree gushes into the air,
A mass of deep oils anchored in clouds
Of gradually rising stairs.

Though the sky is unencumbered, I had felt
The darkness in my hair as a sense
Of wrongness, I had loved wind for its
Hazel and black skin.

For the yellow-lit tunnel of its movement,
For the breaking ribbon of its snake-painted
Eyes. On my feet I painted pretend-
Sandals, my hair

Tried to be red and my skin almost
Turquoise, I put green paint on my upper
Arm, as if it were a plant for the neck,
Or my dry shoulders.

The room took on the feeling of skin,
As the invisible scent-chambers of roses,
Or spongy wood infested with high notes,
Their death gave me

My father's death, and a new kind of winter.
My way was barred by a series
Of flesh beams, the white was blue-white,
White on a blue ground,

But I carried over the segments of colour
Into the background, a swirling, soft
And open colour, that clicked around
In a circle,

That dissolved and thrust forward
Simultaneously and consecutively,
Like a heatwave, never foretold,
Ageing the lily-ceiling

Of the snow. There were signs of overtalk
On the laprobe that covered my knees,
The strength of the two downstrokes
Was staked down

And held firm beneath the opaque clothing.
You beat your hands together, and the huge
Hooded fireplace made a C-shaped
Gesture out of shock.

There are no words, there are reds
In the farthest of my three rooms,
The sound of red when he kisses me once
And the inner mouth shows inside the other.

Amsterdam Avenue

If you exist, make me blue,
You are blue in my picture.
Your eyes are the one thing now
Worth visiting, they take me
Into a winter whose expensive fruit
Outwinters even the winter.

Both brown and ash-grey, dark silver,
Like a candle flaring up
And burning out at the same moment,
A light grey line surrounds
Both irises at their outer door,
A finger dipped in spilt wine
Writing the time on the table.

As if I had been putting out a fire
And caught my death of cold,
Or had been led through one room
Into a second, simple, square,
That I hardly disturbed but filled
Completely, I wore one skirt
On top of another, scarves above
And below, my hair in a tangle
Of combs and pins, suggesting
Don't undress me:

Though my clothes open out like fans
And when it snows I open my mouth
To swallow it. A smile blew in
With the evening from the street,
Your smile, my smile, floated about
On its own, flew around high up
In a circle, melted away to the left.

I press my ten fingers to the hedges
Of my mouth, because you loved me
As if I were a bird, on the edge of the chair;
And the chair isn't mine, the chair
Without a room, the walls are yours,
Lying flat on the ground,
The acute angles of your arms and body.

If there were a hiding-place in my picture
I would slip you into it, your flesh turned
Into paints, your body into a brush.
The way your eyes shone
Was an uncarpeted, dark-oak floor,
An oil-mill trickling down inside me.

It was the moon's occultation of Aldebaran,
That beautiful, fixed star in the sign of Aries.
In the distance your hand drew
A very distinct '2'. I can still see
That number swinging round towards me
And dropping away like a piece of gauze
From a wound.

As though the house had fainted
At the 'A' I fell asleep,
And in what I suppose was a dream,
I was about to go downstairs
From a round landing where a dozen
Numbered doors opened like scissors,
But he would not allow it,
My crooked sheet of paper hummed
Lilac, over the pulse of blue.

The Unplayed Rosalind

for Anne Devlin

July presides, light with a boy's hat,
Dressed in black with his feet on a cushion,
His voice-print is too dry for the stage.

The long-stemmed flowers comparatively
Rained, and the tumultuous sea was making me
Sterile, as though a hand from within it
Slowly drove me back, we were small objects
On its edge.

The telegraph pole sang because a horseshoe
Brushed its foot, and a spider's web darkened
On my finger like a kiss that has to be paid
With the veil lowered, a sweet-sour kiss through tight-
Bitten lips that could make me drunk.

I have lived on a war footing and slept
On the blue revolution of my sword;
Given the perfect narrative nature of blue,
I have been the poet of women and consequently
Of the young; if you burned my letters
In the soiled autumn they would form two hearts.

The room which I thought the most beautiful
In the world, and never showed to anyone,
Is a rose-red room, a roseate chamber.
It lacks two windowpanes and has no waterjug.
There is red ink in the inkwell.

Upstairs above my head lives someone
Who repeats my movements with her double
Weeping. My heart beats as though it were

Hers, and sometimes I have her within my clothes
Like a blouse fastened with a strap.

She moved in her dream, she lost her dream,
She stretched her arms and tossed her head
As a river burrows its bed till the bed burns.
Her dress reminded me of curtains torn
Like a page from a bedroom window.

There was a rustle in the lock of the door,
A noise like grasshoppers as though a great
Moth were caught in it. Then the door
Simply waved, and a long white sheet
Of paper came gliding from under it,
Like a coaster shoved beneath everyone's
Wineglass, or glass being cut under water.

In her there was something of me which
He touched, when she lay on his arm like the unknown
Echo of the word I wanted to hear
Only from his mouth; she spoke words to him
I had already heard.

She said, 'This is too bright for me',
Preferring to see the fire-red rip down heaven
As a saucer of iced water where she could
Dip her hands, as in the reciprocal blue
Ashes of his eyes.

She kissed him as if he were her child
Like a gull rubbing its beak against
A jagged window, and my body felt
All its gossip's knots being traced.

She removed the rose from my mouth
Like the taste of fruit or a button left
On the top of a cupboard. Though she swore
That she did not carry
Another man's child under her heart,
My seed is a loose stormcoat
Of gold silk, with wide sleeves, in her uterus.

Lac de Galance

The three worlds of your hand,
Your earth-hand, water-hand, your
Unsubstantial hand, are woven afresh
Into the texture of this world.

I had seen you hold your thumb
Against your palm, each phalange of each
Finger shut away like a curtain
Of low trees at the horizon.

I had watched the blur of spiral
Fluting on the glass pitcher, the seamless
Rhythms of the sea in your gait, and wanted
To leave, in the way anyone

Here wants anything; the air seemed
Firmer than the calmest sea. The raking
Light of your hair was such a fugitive
Colour, I spun my red sun-hut like

A distracted child after your turned-away
Figure, wondering what you saw.
The pull of my brush was two full inches
From the point where it ought to be

When a cloud of letters chose the moment
Of deepest sleep to burst their white ribbons
Into the same 'M' room. I discovered your name
There among the 'E's

And felt your breathing begin again
Though your face was still hidden
Like the cross on my fingertip
Under the chapter headed 'Touch'.

But the silken rush of your kiss
Was the origin and continuum of sea-water,
Which had never before happened in daylight.
You in grey are my masterpiece.

East of Mozart

Snow gleams like an old leaven
In one corner of my room, a feeling
With no name in actual language,
Which perhaps does not exist except in me.

The room is also filled with white lilac
And looks into the lime trees, as I look first
At your fingers, then at your face,
Through the scalloped marzipan curtains,
Through the lens of poetry.

The garden where the humus begins
Is shorn away, embedded in my memory
As in a block of ice, and time is at once
A toy river running the wrong way,
And a little rain that sends us into the house,
Spelling a cul-de-sac.

The bouquet on my table I can see
Without looking makes me ill,
Its flowers beyond music as they are almost
Beyond poetry will be taken away
To be sold at half-price.

Why is there this why? When every room
Expresses a state of mind,
And I am in the same room as last February,
Where August somehow lodged itself,
And autumn's small sum now meets
As much of my own blood and ink
As will fit into an outsize envelope.

This room again under the roof
Seems an octagonal library,

A silence between past and future
Whose roads, because frozen, are passable.

I live outside a society
Which is itself outside these things,
And anyone can see in the rented fixity
Of my orphaned furniture that it is
Wrongly placed but too heavy to move.

My warped seaside piano opens like winter,
Its un-music, anti-music makes love to me
Till I am music's stepchild,
Music's drudge.

It punctures all its balloons
As fast as they are released, like exhausting
Dreams. Its melody divides between
Two outnumbered hands, as if a man's
Ten fingers could swell like a pedal
And sting like blurted speech.

The sound of it has counted
Every step of the staircase,
And once, when a piece of paper
Fell upon the keys, it went on
Playing through the paper.

It sounds like a thirst for a long sleep;
It represents the cousin
Or the mirror of a kingdom
That nobody believes in.

But some words like some notes
That never pronounce themselves,

Are meant for at most
Ten people in the whole world
Whose oxygen is storms.

If something very young
That does not imitate my touch
Touched me like a ship and sprinkled
Blood over the dust in the night,
My new player would vanish
Into a building without a past.

Echo-Poem

The soul beats
Against the sites of love,
Or childhood,
Like a heart,
Like port
In a claret glass.

And everything red
Is beautiful —
It is so light,
It has such
A warm curve.

Death is heavy-footed,
Bedfast; I feel
Sought by her,
I meet her
In the darkest part
Of staircases,
In regions where time
Can be accurately kept.

She will choose
Her body freely,
As a word chooses
Its meaning,
Her shoulder-twist
And cleavage feeds
Some foam-born
Germ in me.

Now that I have kissed
Her sound awake,
She alliterates
With my father,

She unmoors him; though
I modify
His name by fond
Diminutives, she ties
Him to her stern.

I touch the foxglove
Curtains with my tongue,
And find them salt.
They fall into five
Acts, flinging
A chessman into
The hollow course
Of the window.

Could my Norse
Ancestresses
Praise the Christian
Colour of the sea
In their subtle
War-odes, their impetuous
Songs of occupation,

As the greyest
Of all blue things,
The bluest
Of all grey,
The tear without labour
Which is the straightest-limbed
Daughter of the eye

Would link two wings
Inside a large china brooch
Of fivefold crimson —

The different noises made
By the morning and the night;
The velocity of male
And female clouds.

The Partner's Desk

Yesterday was a gift, a copy of the afternoon,
A heavily wrapped book, a rolled manuscript.
Its paper was buff with blue lines, the sheets
Ragged at the top, and not quite legal size.
It was secured on three sides by green ribbons
Like a wooden tongue of land or the leafy miles
Of a ribbon-maker and, whether it was a letter
He withheld from me, I swore to seal it through death.

The colour is deep enough by itself to make
The children pray for the dead; it is a children's morning.
I arranged the Christmas tree in its green outfit,
Producing its green against the grey sky like handwriting
That has been traced over or, when snow tires us,
The sunshine inside and out of my birthday dove.
Both our birthdays are today, and I was playing with
Its feather on the bed as if it were a brake

On the thawing weather, that almost-summer
Had already arrived. Being still in the grip
Of a dream of pearls which robbed me
Of my un-English language (yesterday
He dreamed of laburnums). It is his December,
Though the wine is May's, and we should keep birds
Only in winter, as we burn the winter
In our curse-laden, extinguished Christmas tree.

Everything I do passes through a narrow door,
And the door seems rather heavy. When I play
The piano my eyes turn brown; it is not a matter
Of eyes, it is something darker than eye-colour,
And we are all part of it. When I teach the continents
To my favourite daughter, my father is there
Though I do not see him. His mood is towards evening.
He asks the bird how many years he has to live,

Or how long the hours will continue to strike.
How very deliberately the bird breaks off,
Praising the stillness. He compares this cry
With his outward appearance, he strokes the veins
On the back of his left hand and extends
His fingers, he looks up at the ceiling
And down at the floor, he feels in his breast
Pocket and pulls a green pamphlet out,

Saying, 'The finest summer I can ever remember
Produced you,' and I remember a second,
Gentler dream, of my wedding year,
Where we took a walk across loose stones,
And he took my hands and stretched them out
As if I were on a cross, but not being punished.
You know the renewed rousing of your fingers
In a dream, your hand glides through the air,

They are not fingers at all. He will leave me
The school clock, the partner's desk, the hanging
Lamp, the head bearing the limbs, as I will leave her
The moonphase watch and the bud vase. I restart
My diary and reconstruct the days. I look upon
The life-bringing cloud as cardboard
And no reason for the life of another soul, yet still
Today is the true midsummer day.

Swallows' Wood, Glenshesk

You are a birdmaker, you coax these sounds
Out of me, stone-checker, wheatear.
In the twist of your arm like the bend
Of a tree, I ease up the skin to make a cut
For the New Year to enter you sleeping.
But it finds us still awake, it comes
As an awakener, like spring and its longing.

When you opened the glass door, summer had gone
As if sketched in pencil. It feels in my memory
Like a Good Friday, the sky cleared only
For my birthday, adding an upper voice to it
Like a tablecloth with roses. The circle of a year
Is too small for one not to keep coming back.
Summer does the composing. I dry the roses.

I can see the coming and going, the black-red-gold
When the sky clears after an east wind. If
The unroselike colours hold a world's ending
In store, one would have to call it a beginning,
We do so need a blue sky, we like to wait
Around after goodbyes. I see the sign
Of the cross in window frames and trees

As if we have come to a border where
A seed which has not arrived has taken root.
I see coffins being brought into a hall,
More and more of them, wrapped in grey canvas,
And you say it is the best dream, the birthwish,
So that when the day is loosed on us, I try
To turn the morning into a continuation of the dream.

Often I fall asleep with my mouth set
In a blackbird silence, my lips' transgression
Is like water falling into water, it is so full.

As if your room were separated from mine
By several other rooms, you are satisfied
By your sleep as by swimming in a broad
Colourless river which brings you my yes.

We live in the sort of house a child
Would draw, I dream I am your sister,
We play with our wedding rings till
I am wearing yours. A mysterious sheltering
House with a school garden — you take it
As far as the kiss and then break off,
Though who would see our foliage-dark kisses?

Did the river bring you the kiss I gave him
For you, his cold music astounded by
Its violence? The wrestle of your sleep
Is a sort of music, your full-blooded eyes
Lowered to death as a tone is lowered
For a question. You say I will die simply,
Without noticing it, like a twig on a tree.

But I feel sad to possess an additional
Ending, I don't want the sideways rain
To cover his face when I wave to him.
Chance brings three lights into my room,
A male bird to my feeding ledge,
The suppressed fire of the roses you particularly
Like, the 'N' sound of evening walking past

In her differing greens, her soul ploughed
So thoroughly by the late-opening shop
Of the sky, a sound emerged
Of more land than I felt would ever end.

Storm-Flap

for Maureen Salters

A wintry look came back to me
And all that now remains of spring
Wants me to tell it things.

Telling you later means it will be
Deeper, no dream can be told
Quite as it was, I am asking
Someone else to be it with me.

Finding him light as a feather,
Exactly the winter one always
Wishes for and now cannot bear.

We give up all thought
Of summer or autumn, feeling
The weather listening inside
The house to something he cannot hear.

Day, our blue protection, has not yet
Come between us, the sea and sky
Are the same dreamier colour
Of dark gardens.

I put into a kiss all the pain
Of three seasons, the heavy flight
Of a breath which would form
With the ending of the world.

I knew the wide page
Would be difficult, I pulled
The glass away from four voices.

But beforehand, a dream
Had confronted me, though I did not
Recognise its blue, so swiftly arisen,

And sent a message of remembrance
To the night behind it,
Without a garden, without a view,
The sky altered and clouds everywhere.

Turning the Moon into a Verb

A timeless winter
That wants to be now
Will go on taking shape in me.
Now everything can begin.

Everything can reach much
Further up; with this new
Listening, the longing at the window
For the missing season weakens.

When springtime had need of him,
He did not offer me the winter,
He took away each of the seasons
In its visual turn.

Dark does that to you also,
And the headlessness
Of a turning of light that mentions a green
A little darker than all other greens.

A secret year, a secret time,
Its flight is a written image
Of its cry, its capacity for sound
I call spring, the experience

When the sky becomes a womb,
And a vision of rivers slanting
Across the doubly opened page
Of the moon turns her into a verb.

An image I have consciously
Broken like a shoulder on your hearing,
The inconstancy within constancy
That is the price of a month.

Earth Weather

My sight is so overladen with the seen world,
I would like to wash that too-small touch from my eyes.
Uncomprehended, darkness begins a sky in some eyes
As sleep pretends to enter a house with twilight,
A step towards black, letting the colours arise.

The pure colour of my mornings are a birthday.
I contain a face like water, I collect its light in a bowl.
My dream goes to its hands, they allow themselves to be
    dreamed,
I hold it without hands, then a hand opens with the coldness
Of a boy's hand, and lets something go.

I thought winter would adopt me like a conception
Of coolness, draw me like linen through a ring,
And let me recover beneath you. But my dress
Is heavy as stone, my lips have not moved into any evening,
The sound which was ours has a different body.

When a window holds itself in a still wider forgetting
To the imaginary mouth of the storm, I move on
My moist light to the next window, drinking its changes
Until it is dark. Will spring find me divided like a door
Shared half with you and half with the forest?

Unforgettable, with fragments of sleep in their faces,
The trees come back from the pulp of March.
The distance folds their roots like feathers, in the round space
Of fear remains a visible sky whose outward turning
Wards off all things.

Branches

This window, clumsily inserted,
Was originally a door.
So am I detached
From the fabric which claims me.

Under one rain, the same rain,
I sleep two dreams in one,
And am softened like a touch
Blurred by a curtain.

My eyes are so diffused with blood,
I see it and say it
And only expect it, my veins
Are powerful as open arms.

I curve my three middle fingers inwards
Like the larch in the stairs;
I force the closely written page
To bend me, as though it had created me.

Slow-forming, the most changeable of all,
Sky on sky in crescent-like sequence
Overcomes the touch of another,
Intertwines hedgelessly with the garden.

And brings its shape to bear twice over
On only one of our hours, unrelieved,
Loaded down like a bookshelf,
And content with bearing, nothing else.

Sky-Writing

Being seen like this by you,
A steeply perched, uplooking town,
Am I the same in a more strengthened way?
Can another afternoon belong
To such a morning? When will the evening
Be itself again, and who?

What can I do against this room
I was obliged to let grow and grow
In the new space all through the winter?
October dawns seeking the distance
Of their unfolding are startled
By a vessel so restricted holding them.

I forfeit the world outside
For the sake of my own inwardness,
I am so at one with the scent of its many wills:
Its inexhaustible innocency
Lapses past me like a future not lived strongly,
I abandon myself to its incubative weight.

I am on the point of falling
Like the essence of rain or a letter
Of ungiveable after-love into the next degree
Of spring, its penultimate tones:
Shall I ever again be caught up gently
As the rustle of a written address by the sky?

Open Rose

The moon is my second face, her long cycle
Still locked away. I feel rain
Like a tried-on dress, I clutch it
Like a book to my body.

His head is there when I work,
It signs my letters with a question-mark;
His hands reach for me like rationed air.
Day by day I let him go

Till I become a woman, or even less,
An incompletely furnished house
That came from a different century
Where I am a guest at my own childhood.

I have grown inside words
Into a state of unbornness,
An open rose on all sides
Has spoken as far as it can.

Venus and the Sea

When I return from poetry as from a sea-shore
To the streets of dream, what is left on waking
Is whatever I was full of, naming itself:
'A colour walks around, with people hidden in it.'

A summer that was meant to mean nothing
Lifted his ten fingers like a fence between us
Or snow that does not fall. I felt him through
An envelope, a glove touching a glove.

His sound-curves so quivering, I was shorn
Of all words, and hummed him with my eyes
And mouth. The incomplete opening of his mouth
Lives in my hand like a wound, the thought

Of the subtraction and the narrowing circle
Is like a turn-of-the-century spring along
A delayed fuse or a graph of deep
Confusions, reaching the first trees.

It begins in an hour like the door-mirror
Of a wardrobe cracking the memory
Of an over-remembered window-door

Wiping off the painted pinpoint pupils
And the ringlets of music with a smile
Waking in the separate mouth beside me.

D

The War Ending

In the still world
Between the covers of a book,
Silk glides through your name
Like a bee sleeping in a flower
Or a seal that turns its head to look
At a boy rowing a boat.

The fluttering motion of your hands
Down your body presses into my thoughts
As an enormous broken wave,
A rainbow or a painting being torn
Within me. I remove the hand
And order it to leave.

Your passion for light
Is so exactly placed,
I read them as eyes, mouth, nostrils,
Disappearing back into their mystery
Like the war that has gone
Into us ending;

There you have my head,
A meeting of Irish eyes
With something English:
And now,
Today,
It bursts.

Charlotte's Delivery

for Pat Taylor

1

Summer never really came, its false hem
Beneath the quiet dress of shadow
Half-in, half-out of the rainwashed dream.

Something in its rounded winter power
Expanding for a bold internal minute
Made me decide on giving her a cold, short name.

Will it be stained as darkly as the last,
The tiny tapering of the inverted cup,
The faintly printed journey out of the mourning brooch?

2

Your morning sounds are a womb of roses,
Sinking into life and who-ness.
You collect yourself against me like a first book of time,
Dipping in and out of a coma.

You are a ring with a love-note hidden inside:
The us-ness in your eyes is what men, who are not us, go
   to find.
In the wrecked hull of the fishing-boat
Someone has planted a cypress under the ribs.

Breaking the Blue

Deluged with the dustless air, unspeaking likeness:
You, who were the spaces between words in the act of reading,
A colour sewn on to colour, break the blue.

Single version of my mind deflected off my body,
Side-altar, sacramental, tasting-table, leaf to my
Emptying shell, heart with its aortic opening,

Your mouth, my dress was the scene that framed
Your shut eye like hands or hair, we coiled
In the lifelong snake of sleep, we poised together

Against the crevice formed by death's forefinger
And thumb, where her shoulder splits when desire
Goes further than the sender will allow.

Womb-encased and ever-present mystery without
Release, your even-coloured foliage seems a town garden
To my inaccessible, severely mineral world.

Fragments of once-achieved meaning, ready to leave
The flesh, re-integrate as lover, mother, words
That overwhelm me: You utter, become music, are played.

Oval of a Girl

The summers of our house peel and rot.
Sunset has begotten them, thinking he could shut
It in with varnish. But one discarnate shadow
Can be worth a whole generation; I am flooded
By no ocean but a second you.

Who might just as well have been water
Breaking and mending with a dark little movement,
A kind of forlorn frenzy leaking over into sound,
For whose unpronounceable blue I am an ear,
Alerted, stretching, not as I had prayed.

I have a hundred ways of turning
This year of the world's redemption
Into an ominous nativity, a face too fast
And fallen, too formed and fresh to seem asleep,
Already soiled by this eye-opening winter.

Near-child, much-needed, present tense,
Your first grown-up spring is under wordless control,
Beyond poetry, like a poem of the deepest calm
Never to be written, or a city re-beguiled
By useless fields that were all but air to me.

From the First Underworld

Being able to know colour
Lacks all colour. I am following
This black thread
Stretched across the stairs
As if to kiss me again.

The sun shines through my sleep
Like a man in a coma
Or a seed left by an earlier mind
Sown in a natural body:
Has my will kindled to itself this light?

I have been called nothing
For so long, I only know
One of his names, though men can
Make a name of two names,
And both are deathless.

Unless I am my soul,
The brightness of your decay
Rises up from an opening in a dining-table
And gives me a flower
White with a tincture of red

Like the damask rose.
And it is not the semi-soul
Of a neo-nate in its uncontrolled dreaming,
Or the listening behaviour
Of 'mere foam, aura or melody',

But such an ensouled thing
As if you had died
Fighting in a holy war
For some inert and unobtrusive God.
My wholly this-worldly question,

Without end though not without beginning,
Is whether, with the possibility of cruelty,
We are indeed such choice creatures
Or clouds within hesitation quotes
Felt, heard, finding the imageless air.

The Carrying Ring

for Joan and Kate Newman

It waits until it is discovered
Like a part of nature which cannot just
Wait patiently, but must wait forever.

As the seen room is also the field
Of a biography, as the conceived or recollected
Room is the beginning of a life.

We do not love these ingredients
That make up the obscured moment
Keenly enough, our words increase the darkness,

And no word closes our quest,
Truth happens to them after all the truths
Have straightened themselves out together.

Feelings are like colours, which cannot hold
Fragments in place, but one experience
Can know another, and one part lean on another,

Though experience leans on nothing.
The odour of these silences frightens me
Like time, because it works out the problem:

How to come to desire
What suddenly leaves us so alone,
A protecting obedience so contrary to human love,

Where the visible is the carrying ring
For the invisible. Each languageless flake
Of that night-filled mountain is a sleep

And all that labour is to have
An awareness of one's being
Added to one's being, like a first daughter:

The cloudy, the overcast, then
Something shone upon.

The After-Thinker

The brightest dark in the world
Is your shadow thinned to light:
Your eyes, before they are hearse horses,
Are two unused theatre tickets;
Eternal, lifeless, going under the gathered knowledge
That they are not real, they are merely filled time.

When you are sunlight you will take
Eight minutes to cross to my window;
When your repeated figurative deaths
Become a wardrobe of fragrances,
I will call up the honey-stain of love like a seat
Around a sycamore, or a halo of very old stars.

Since I lack every relation with you now
But the deepest, give me a conscience
One fourth as bright that will teach me
'-tion' and '-ness'; let my secluded ego
Be a parenting melody or sheltering leaves
Through that narrow passage of re-birth:

Impulse of water in your path,
Starfire locked in your starfield,
Winter or evening perfume over your square of space,
Congregation of dust, in whose self-divesting push
I become so rich that God is not enough for me,
The gender of your unconditional 'alive'.

Almond

Houses show more now
Among the bare trees,
Grains of thought exposed
To the thinking stars.

Oaks hardly seen in summer
Give the prevailing hue,
Where every colour is a food,
And the sun feeds upon blue.

Dark ice on the dead leaves
Lies faint and adorable,
So imperiously pure without
The intervening water.

And I feel I could get into time
If I wished,
Where lands widen out
On a round planet

And advance to meet,
Bearing in their bodies
The weight of the moving world.
There is something imperishable

Even in the in and out
Of their breathing,
That irreducible
Quality of createdness.

The something not God
That is the ocean,
The soul of souls
Collecting all the streams,

Has, itself, a far less
Developed face,
And a heart heard by an ear
Far less subtle.

To be worked
To an almond shape,
At the cost of an apparent death,
To follow the road

On which we lose the power
Of explaining ourselves
Back ever more deeply
Is to mix in the earth

Or soil as a ferment,
To redissolve the hazards
Of our own growth
Like the very flower of matter

Woven into the common ground.
From the earliest bed
To this final granting of shelter
Is no dismemberment,

But summer returning in her
Presentation dress,
Pre-living light
On bare places on the shoulders

From the desert of the sky,
The absorbent bones
In their cold association
Seeing morning within.

She Which Is Not, He Which Is

An elm box without any shape inscribed
Like a tool in the closed vessel of the world;
I will be flat like a dream on both sides,
Or a road that makes one want to walk.

My words will be without words
Like a net hidden in a lake,
Their pale individual moisture.
My eyes will not be the eyes of a poet
Whose voice is beyond death;
This face, these clothes, will be a field in autumn
And the following autumn, will be two sounds,
The second of which is deeper.

The sky for me on any one night
Will be the successive skies over the course
Of a year, for time that I love
Will have cut up and entered my body;
Time will have gathered the roots
Of my last spring, floating rather
Than anchored, and thrust them between
The two planes of my cheek and brow.

Even now, his lips are becoming
Narrower and bloodless, ever-searching,
Razor-like; unforgettable time,
During which I forget time, a new sort
Of time that descends so far down
Into me and still stays pure.

I imagine his house as a possible setting
For the harmony between one drop of water
And another, one wave and another wave,
Where the light accustoms one to light
And each occurrence is a touch.

When we pass through some darkness,
The waiting has pulled us.
Without the help of words, words take place.

Compared with this absence, weighed,
Diluted in time, presence is abandonment,
Absence his manner of appearing,
As though one received from outside
The energy to accept the swept room
As much as the sweeping.

Though each instant of light
Wipes away a little of it,
We shall not lose the way
In which things receive it:

Carry me who am death
Like a bowl of water
Filled to the brim
From one place to another.

Vibratory Description

When we make nature over again,
The experience not bright, the thought not red,
The soul being a substance cannot explain
Just that red as felt in the room or bed:

Or how the rest of the merely understandable
World, whose art of persistence is to be dead,
Enters like twilight perched in her disrobing
The more with which we are connected.

It was four-thirty by the car clock, thought
Rested, thought hurried on, sorry to be awake,
And the room kept too much of you, as part
Of the history of the house, the withness of your body,

The here of your mind, the awareness
Of the silence, the form of the sentence yet to come.
Many separate causes poured a kind of aimless
Weather into the meaning at its widest,

At the width where it is lost, among things
Greater than itself. Real losses and real losers,
We find them possessing us, but if paths
Are irradiated at all, that stays numbered

Whose coherence is all we ever ask for,
One surface re-youthing another by its fact,
And the objects in the indescribable background
Who did all that lay within them.

In the Rainshadow

Reposing traveller, ready to see the willow pattern streets,
My days settle down on their blurred desires
Like every breathing animal or star.
Air, filler of all, that used to be
A coldness in my mouth,
Brings a sense of young commotion in the older weather,
Like a hand bared waiting for mine to touch —
To gaze me into feeling here,
To re-seal me in place,
Missing the smell of being unvisited in the garden.

The months clipped off mingle
With the news-gathering year;
I have had two springs, one bright, one dark:
One that seemed a sky away from August,
Without the sparks of poems,
Whose climbing yellow light protected me
Like a whole city of looks;
And one that gives my head a chance
To listen back and speak to the other,
Where though I was a sentence unattached
To its noun, in my tight-made bed,
Whatever I clouded was warm.

An arriver in a land, it was I
Who was passing, not the world,
The world-flight lost me,
It was too foreign a search.
Every road had my fallen art by the shoulders.
What I say now takes the different sound
That ran under me, a few inches from music,
Voice like dry wood whose fire
Was hidden like a child greedy in the womb.

Family of then to the emptiest of trains,
What most wishes itself unsaid
Or nine waves out to the sea.

Do I go on till summer
In my own strip of the night,
While night falls into its two halves
Behind the rain-curtains?
And the light of day at each end
Is only the delayed echo,
The dying and recovery
Of this so-travelled sound,
The carrying of the stage-voice
Arm in arm with the breeze,
Without the actual foothold of a single word,
When darkness immortalizes itself
As in a window,
And half the room is bared
In a heart-pause of moonlight?

Heart, you torn postcard, here it is,
Newspaper I've been trying to open in the wind,
Companion, messenger,
Undifferentiated seed of the lightest colour,
Invisibility,
So-soon-cold lake flowing in my veins,
Moon laden with the moisture of three sets of ashes,
My muddy pairing wrung out downward
At the deepest moral note where people
Can still press together
What they both remember
Till it joins.

Flowered Sitting-room

Your low-roofed half-kitchen half-parlour
Old type of motherhood loses the sun.
Two field-lengths from the house, your snow-white
Companion, morning, makes the land more silent
Than if we had never heard of him.

You touch one of his bitten apples
With your lips not soft,
Almost without thinking of the first signs
Of winter breaking up; in your heart's heart,
This is your world for the moment.

Daily before your eyes, for three
Short, long months, a flower
That looks thick, round and double
Faces a gradual death:

But what is your experience of the flower,
If not a vision so absolutely untransferable,
That when early summer (now our newest neighbour)
Colours his evening kiss with your resting-place,
You see in him the impersonation of dawn?

The Snow Speaker

So little of the earth, you
Open the earth for me.

Having no more need of me
Than I of you,
I am as alone with you
As without you.

I try to love the sky
As the sea's accomplice,
But nothing human
Can help us know the stars.

Threshing a poem
Or a grape-harvest
Takes four equal limbs
And a horizontal cutting
That has always already begun.

You are speaking of
That wholly woven day,
Not stunning, nor bitter.

Your pleasure just fits
On the postcard of evening;
An envelope would have given off
Too sharp a smell.

Another room closes
The door of the sun
And gathers carefully
All the water that falls.

Sky in Narrow Streets

Rose posing in air-hungry water
With a duellist's stance:

Sky so disordered by decomposing colours
It takes light from the house:

Unhellenised moon, harsh yellow petticoat
Lined with red, prevents the leaves from moving.

My watercolour of trees, seascapes at dawn,
Noon and night, the unmade furniture of earth,
Promise to pay what is never going to be kept.

I am a knife-rest or a spoon-rest
For your winter's love, the hollow bitten
Into the midday dream of your address.

I drive words abreast
Into the interior of words;
It is murder or kindling when two meanings
Rush together from such a distance,
No multiplicity can distress them.

There is a month that can take care
Of itself, there are flowers
That go on opening down the stalk:

When I have over-yellowed the parchment
From the honey of my walls,
Or added a living shape to my bowl of deads,
There is a lovebird green between the tree-roots
So transparent, it is the flowers that are obedient.

This needed gleam, as one comes out
From the supreme surrender of an arch,
The relative silence of a kissing sound,

Is from the tree being seen
In a different place in the garden,
And everything I had thought about trees, nowhere.

Red Armchair

November will dance his night-journey towards me,
Playing his headlamps in a round robin
From leaf to target-leaf.

September will close the eyes of October's fever;
If my father dies in the wasted arms of summer,
The sudden warm flood of his melted life
Will make new constellations.

Like black and white flowers, family photographs
Sparkle to distract death's attention back to love.
May refuses and June extorts
His purple kiss, fog-bound in a restaurant,
Wet with towels in a frosted bathroom.

Through the cornfield above the hawthorn path,
There is a planter's or a trout-fisherman's lodge
Which could also be the studio of two artists:
One stitches a red arboreal background
To the other's marine imagery,
With the perfection of the unseen body,
Into his voice.

Marconi's Cottage

Small and watchful as a lighthouse,
A pure clear place of no particular childhood,
It is as if the sea had spoken in you
And then the words had dried.

Bitten and fostered by the sea
And by the British spring,
There seems only this one way of happening,
And a poem to prove it has happened.

Now I am close enough, I open my arms
To your castle-thick walls, I must learn
To use your wildness when I lock and unlock
Your door weaker than kisses.

Maybe you are a god of sorts,
Or a human star, lasting in spite of us
Like a note propped against a bowl of flowers,
Or a red shirt to wear against light blue.

The bed of your mind has weathered
Books of love, you are all I have gathered
To me of otherness; the worn glisten
Of your flesh is relearned and reloved.

Another unstructured, unmarried, unfinished
Summer, slips its unclenched weather
Into my winter poems, cheating time
And blood of their timelessness.

Let me have you for what we call
Forever, the deeper opposite of a picture,
Your leaves, the part of you
That the sea first talked to.

Teraphim

Deathly nameless angel, bend to my earth:
When you speak as fire should,
We become sweet water.
I wait for you like a road,
Without quite knowing that you wait,
My openness is like a name
Whose root you play on to say only
Something about yourself.

But only you can take me back
Beyond yourself, only you
Can change me by overhearing you speak.

When an earlierness,
Now forever forsaken,
Either way kisses us,
Like a natural radiance,
Or a story we were not born into,

Two paths we cannot distinguish between
Fold us into the lost
Strangeness of our namelessness,

The mist in which we are swallowed
Allows a garden to be planted,
To breathe with our breath.

Is it just this difference
That makes a difference,
Is it my name that you, more than a person,
Need or ask?

In the time a meaning ripens from your face,
An anxiety of touch and sight you cannot fill
Finds us in the garden we have felt before
That makes itself, where even the ground speaks.

Time-Words

I am a debt, soon I will be added,
As words wither away with the things they describe,
As clouds may catch each other up,
As now is overtaken and tomorrow is an 'I'.

Saying 'we' is dangerous, like time-words without soul.
I must have met them yesterday and loved their hunger.
The sea lives in the present so the present exists
In its waters like a heart not made to be broken.

Light is wider than time, it is I love,
It gives up being everything to become a view,
Like an emerald uncreating itself
To be green predominating in a skirt.

And the kiss is to turn the light back,
As though burnt or exhausted by its touch;
It is the theft when it has vanished,
And dark feels, what part of it was loved?

On Her Second Birthday

for Emer Mary Charlotte Rose

In the beginning I was no more
Than a rising and falling mist
You could see through without seeing.

A flame burnt up the paper
On which my gold was written,
The wind like a soul
Seeking to be born
Carried off half
Of what I was able to say.

It seems as though
To explain the shape of the world
We must fall apart,
Throw ourselves upon the world,
Slip away from ourselves
Through the world's inner road,
Whose atoms make us weary.

Suddenly ever more lost
Between the trees
I saw the edge of the forest
Which had no end,
Which I came dangerously close
To accepting for my life,

And followed with my eye a shadow
Floating from horizon to horizon
Which I mistook for my own.
It grew greater while I grew less,
Gliding like a world, a tapestry
One looks at from the back.

The more it changed
The more it changed me into itself,
Till I regarded it as more real
Than all else, more ardent
Than love. Higher than the air
Of a dream,
A field in which I ripened
From an unmoving, continually nascent
Light into pure light.

My contours can still
Just be made out, in the areas of fragrance
Of its power over me.
A slight tremor betrays
The imperfection of the union
In its first surface.

But I flow outwards till I am something
Belonging to it and flower again
More perfectly everywhere present in it.
It believes in me,
It cannot do without me,
I know its name:
One day it will pass my mind into its body.

Acknowledgements and Notes

Acknowledgements are due to the editors of the following publications in which some of these poems have appeared: *Antaeus*, *Common Knowledge*, *Force 10*, *The Honest Ulsterman*, *The Irish Review*, *Maryland Poetry Review*, *Numbers*, *Orbis*, *Oxford Poetry*, *Poetry Book Society Anthology*, *Prospice*, *Rhinoceros*, *The Yale Review* and *ZLR*.

page 16   The title is adapted from a statement of Rilke's about the artist Paula Modersohn-Becker.

page 29   In the Russian Orthodox marriage ceremony, 'Shaferi' are the attendants who hold the crowns over the participants.

page 31   'Choorka', one of Tolstoy's pet-names for his daughter, is translated to give the poem its title.

page 42   The title derives from the note-books of the artist Gwen John and signifies the graduated numbers of the spectrum of colours she used.